The Making of an Ideal Boss
by: David Brooke

Work - it's something few of us truly
enjoy and most of us spend the
majority of our lives doing. Select
individuals are handed the thankless
job of supervising the masses of less-
skilled workers; managers, CEOs,
owners, whatever name they go by we
know them all as "bosses". Whether
"work" conjures up visions of an ocean
floor or a Spartan cubicle we all have
one thing in common - if we work, we
either are or have supervisors. Who
are these devoted professionals who
serve as the backbone of the work
force...and better still, how do they do
it?

Throughout my years on the job I have
had a number of bosses ranging from
people with absolutely no supervisory
competence to people who are goal-
oriented and keep their underlings on
track and working efficiently. Then
there are the truly exemplary leaders
who manage to become a member of
their team and promote productivity,
teamwork and job satisfaction. I would
like to take a closer look at each of

these types of supervisors. What made them fit or unfit for their jobs? Above all, what stellar characteristics comprise an ideal supervisor?

A Quick Sketch

Imagine if you will an office building filled with cubicles, each containing keyboards with heads bent over them. Keys tap busily away as the day wears on toward 5:00. Any boss would swell with pride at happening upon such a show of productivity, as well they should. Now let's shake things up a bit and send the supervisor amongst the ranks to check out these proceedings close-up.

Suddenly the cubicles are filled with darting eyes and hands as internet games and e-mail accounts are swiftly shut down, magazines are whisked into desk drawers and a few antsy workers who may have lingered a little too long at the water cooler scurry back to their work stations. The boss - possibly a jowly, aloof gentleman with a somewhat distinguished air...or possibly an ex-drill sergeant or strict matron - strolls through the aisles, turning a sharp gaze on each worker who does not look absorbed enough in their work and dealing out punishment to any slackers.

Sure, work places like this exist everywhere...in the movies. In a true-to-life workplace the employees are neither as lazy nor as fearful as the people in my sketch and the supervisors are neither as impersonal nor as strict. What real-life supervisors are, are real people.

Any given supervisor will hopefully have a strong set of leadership skills offset with a personality that will encourage their employees to confide in them and work alongside them. You would be correct in the observation that this is no easy bill to fill and, sadly, just not enough exemplary individuals to fill all the supervisory positions and so this ideal is rarely achieved, yet through constant improvement and refining I do believe that any responsible person can become an outstanding supervisor.

Bad Traits

Bad traits in a supervisor are often easy to pick out; so many seemingly minor things can greatly affect how that supervisor is perceived and treated in the workplace. We will begin our scrutiny here.

Negative Attitude. This one is a biggie...there's nothing a dissatisfied person would like more than confirmation that they have a reason to be unhappy. If the boss is unhappy that is often construed as sufficient reinforcement for negative behaviors in the workers...after all, non-supervisory employees get paid less, usually have inferior work spaces and less desirable schedules so they must have more reason to complain, right?

Bear in mind these negative attitudes do not necessarily have to be directed at other employees. I am reminded of a particular boss of mine who performed his duties very well, but his frustration was easy to see whenever he was displeased. Even though he never directed the frustration at the people he supervised the attitude still caught on like a bad virus whenever he walked by.

Unpleasant Personality. We're going to take the negative attitude one step further. I'd like to address the supervisors who come across as unfriendly or "rough" to other people. A supervisor may be the most able person in the company with the skills to accomplish twice the work in half the time, but if the other employees are instantly turned off by unnecessarily gruff or rude behavior they simply will not want to be near the person - much less work with them.

Laziness or Perceived Laziness. The cold fact about supervisory positions is that they simply are not fair. You may be the hardest-working boss in the place, but if you spend your entire time doing paperwork or checking orders there is a good chance those you work with will perceive you as being lazy. Alternatively, there are those who actually are lazy. These people have reached their position in the company and have reliable people on their team so they like to kick back and do as little as possible throughout the day. After all, if the other people know what they're doing they don't need close supervision, right? Even if your team runs as smooth as silk there is always room for improvement and areas where your consistent help and support will keep the project moving forward.

Laziness is a difficult stigma to shake as evidenced by a manager in a retail store who spent a large part of his day standing in the aisles with a handheld terminal checking stocking levels. Technically this manager was doing his job, but a part of his job that did not necessarily require so much attention and left a lot more physical work for everyone else. To those of us he was supposed to be supervising the constant routine of standing in the aisles and sitting in the break room definitely appeared lazy. This perception of laziness can inspire disrespect and the feeling that the boss doesn't know what he's doing.

Acting Aloof with the Members of Your Team. I have seen this scenario numerous times...someone gets promoted to manager, it goes to their head and suddenly they think they are better than everyone else and act accordingly. In my own experience there is nothing quite as discouraging as an aloof supervisor; these people do not mingle with their team or make themselves easily approachable.

In this case the likelihood of questions being asked when needed and priorities or expectations being properly communicated is fairly slim. We can't all appear open to every person but a good supervisor can find a way to pave the avenues of communication...which starts with becoming *part* of the team, not just the leader of it.

Good Traits

In my mind the following traits are not just nice to have, they are essentials to being a good boss; the lack of any one of these can be a serious handicap to a person's supervisory capabilities. Obviously there are many other traits that are positive attributes to a supervisor but for the sake of brevity I have included only the ones I feel are the most important.

Recognition of Work. So we're adult, professional people in the work force; we're not in kindergarten and don't expect to be coddled and given gold stars for every little thing done right. That said, we are still human and appreciate feedback on our work...especially positive feedback.

I certainly don't think excessive praise is effective or useful (see **Varying Traits** below) but an occasional "pat on the back" for a job well done goes a long way in encouraging workers to give that fabled 110%. This doesn't have to be just for particular projects where someone did an exceptional job, in fact I think some of the most effective praise is the out of the blue "You know, you really do good work here and we appreciate the effort" which lets non-supervisory employees know they do a good job that is noticed every day.

Outgoing and Conversational. By "conversational" I don't mean a boss that will try to talk to you all day every day or that wastes time chatting up customers or other employees. Rather, I refer to someone who is easy to engage in conversation so when questions or problems arise people feel comfortable bringing their issues to them. In my opinion this is one of the most important traits in a good supervisor.

If your team members don't let you know when there is a problem because they feel you are difficult to talk to it's that much more challenging to keep people satisfied and working efficiently. On the same token, I also refer to "outgoing" in a work-centric way. An outgoing boss is someone who will make sure to introduce themselves promptly to new employees and, more importantly, make it a point to regularly ask non-supervisory employees if they have any concerns or ideas on how things can be done better.

Problem-Solving Skills. "Problem solving" always brings to mind the exercises in high school math class; depending on the type of job you do there is probably no math involved, but a person with a similarly scientific brain has a distinct advantage in the supervisory work force. It doesn't matter what job you have, there is no way to foresee every problem that will come along; I can recall two experiences in particular that taught me just how important it is to be able to "think on your toes" in a supervisory position.

A few years ago I was working in a small department doing a lot of heavy lifting and some specialized tasks. We had a very small team but worked well together and couldn't do it with any less people...until one person had to leave town for several months to take care of family and another hurt his back and had to be transferred to an area where no lifting was required. This left the supervisor with only *me* to work with.

To this day I am amazed at the ways my boss re-organized everything in the department to be able to work it with maximum efficiency so that the two of us could keep everything running smoothly by ourselves for over six months. My second recollection happened a long time ago when I was still quite young...a large sum of money disappeared from the work place in such a way as to look like I did it. My youth and having no prior jobs to vouch for my integrity, combined with the fact that the boss did not know me, would have made it very easy for her to simply go with the obvious conclusion and fire me.

Instead, this particular boss never made any accusatory gestures except to calmly and frankly ask me if I took the money. At my denial she devised a plan to find the real thief. I do not know all the details of the measures she took to solve the mystery, but when the culprit was found the following week I knew I'd be grateful for her efforts the rest of my life.

Where hasty action would have put a nasty blot on my record and given me a negative reference when I was still trying to find my way in the working world, this boss employed ingenuity and effort to ensure the correct person received punishment.

Involvement With and Understanding the Jobs of Your Employees. Obviously a supervisor can't do everything; they have far too much to do with their own jobs to have to worry about doing the jobs of others as well. However, a supervisor must have a basic idea of what their employee's job requires.

There are two obvious reasons the supervisor must be well-acquainted with the jobs of the people they work with. First, if you don't know the work needing done it's pretty difficult to devise a plan for the best way to do it, right? Second, if you don't know all the tasks required of everyone else and the amount of time they should take you're more likely to give a person too much or too little to do.

I have run into this second problem many times in a job that went through supervisors faster than copier paper; the new supervisor often wonders why I am getting so little done until he or she confronts me with something like "how hard is it to _____?" and I tell them all the other things required of my position that they were not aware of. That certainly explains why the couple of things the supervisor thought were all I did didn't get done as quickly as he or she thought it should.

Communicates Expectations. At one time I thought communicating expectations was a given. After the number of supervisors I've had that did not go out of their way to tell non-supervisory employees what to do, I think it does need to be addressed. Referring back to the company that went through an inordinate number of supervisors...my first boss in this job was a shining example of what not to do by way of communication.

In fact, this particular boss didn't really say much at all; she gave each employee a two-hour training orientation which basically consisted of showing them where everything was and how to put items on shelves and then never gave them any additional guidance. I spent nearly a month doing the few things she'd shown me and tripping through all the things she hadn't before a non-supervisory employee from another department asked me why a number of other things had gone untended. You can imagine my immense relief when someone else replaced this person a couple of months later, immediately giving me a list of expectations and making himself available to teach me how to complete them.

Varying Traits

Varying traits are things that can exist in a good supervisor and in some cases may even be a great asset to them, but in other cases can be a severe downfall. These are traits that are often responded to differently by different people. For instance, some supervisors may have a very strict demeanor which can demand respect and make people listen, but that may also cause them to be unlikable enough to certain employees to cause the hesitancy in communication I mentioned before.

One extremely varying trait that comes to mind is the level of supervisory involvement that is most effective with each individual. Personally, I prefer supervisors who deliver their expectations and then back off and let me fulfill those expectations with my own style. This allows me to feel at ease giving complete concentration to my work instead of feeling like I should be paying attention to the other person in the vicinity - my boss. I still expect to be able to find the boss quickly and easily if I have any questions.

Some people may prefer a boss who stays nearby and directs them task-by-task; they may also need someone to keep them focused on the work at hand to be productive. There is little room for a happy medium in this area, each person's preference on the level of supervision is generally pretty set in stone and the "gray area" a supervisor has to work with is small.

Chances are there will be at least some dissatisfied people in a workplace for this reason. The most effective way to strike a balance, in my observation, has been to simply ask each person what they prefer and try to give them their preference as long as the work is being completed to your satisfaction.

Previously I discussed the importance of recognizing an employee's contribution to the company and its positive effects on that employee - now I'd like to discuss the negative effects. It's obvious how a complete lack of recognition or feedback can dishearten an employee by making them feel like their work doesn't mean anything or make them wonder if they're doing their job well or not, but perhaps it's not so obvious how the opposite can also be detrimental.

Praise that is given too freely may come to be considered cheap by the employees, especially if they see people who are not as good at their jobs getting equal recognition. Praise is often a motivator for people to extend themselves in their jobs as much as possible and try to overcome new challenges specifically for the recognition, so if that recognition comes too easy (or not at all) there is little driving incentive for the over-achiever.

One of my best bosses had a very strict demeanor and was often construed as unfriendly by my co-workers; she demanded a lot from everyone and made sure we stayed on task at all times, but what made her one of the best was that every once in a while, for no particular reason, she'd quietly pull someone aside just to tell them they've been doing a good job.

Her personality didn't work for everyone, some preferred to react by becoming hostile or quitting but none ever shirked their duties on the job and most of us warmed up to her and did our best to live up to her expectations. Recognition is one of the most powerful tools a supervisor has and care must be taken to use it but not cheapen it.

In my opinion the most varying trait of all is personality. I've mentioned some desirable personality traits and some other personalities that somehow work despite their unpopularity and personalities that people tend to open up to and ones that shut them down, and all of these have the potential to either work well or backfire. You've heard about clashing personalities - people who just can't get along no matter what they try because for some reason they just get under each other's skin. Sometimes a personality clash can be the fault of one person or the other because of a negative outlook or a simple lack of desire to get along amiably with each other, but so often it's because of no fixable reason. I can think of several bosses whose mere presence set my teeth on edge and I never could determine exactly why I didn't like them.

At least one felt the same about me...why did this happen? Something in our personalities simply did not mesh well. Personality clashes are a constant hazard in the workplace and can happen to anyone no matter how civil or pleasant they are, but often they can be improved over time or at least dealt with in a way that will not be detrimental to the work place.

Deal Killers

Ever have a boss with just one big glaring fault that took your mind away from everything else about them? Namely, these faults take the focus away from what a great, well-organized and effective boss the person is and put the attention on that one negative aspect. Again, there are so many things that can apply to this particular area and we don't have time or space to cover them all so I will just address the ones that I have personally experienced with past bosses.

Hygiene. Yes, hygiene is a real y big deal killer in the workplace. Think back to your past supervisors...was there any one you remember solely because they had messy hair, smelled funny or wore stained clothes? There is one man that I have never met but is the owner of a successful local restaurant.

One would assume that the business's success means he knows what he is doing, yet I know several people that have worked for him that only remember his severe bad breath and the growing dread at the prospect of being called into his office for any reason. It's not always easy to know if you have a hygiene problem that will turn people off but measures can be taken to be as neat and clean as possible.

If you are unsure about whether or not you have a problem in this area then ask a loved one you know will tell you the truth - and be prepared for unpleasant answers.

Attitudes That Turn People Off. As noted about personality clashes it can, unfortunately, be just about any attitude that turns people off - it all depends on who you're dealing with. For me, there was a man who I hated working with for two years before I finally learned to see around his abrupt manner and realize what skills he had to manage and do an outstanding job; many people are not that patient.

These attitudes can be unfriendliness, abruptness, excessive energy...whatever attitude it is there will be someone somewhere who is turned off by it and so have a difficult time working with a supervisor that has that personality type.

Unworthy Expectations. By "unworthy expectations" I mean a boss who consistently underestimates or overestimates an employee's capabilities. There is nothing more aggravating to me than to constantly be in trouble with the higher-ups because some tasks go uncompleted when the daily requirements are simply set too high. Alternatively, if a supervisor always asks too little it is easy to get bored or to feel like the boss has no confidence in your abilities. Striking the proper balance isn't easy and it certainly doesn't happen overnight. It takes constantly revising expectations to make sure a person is getting enough of a challenge but not being overwhelmed.

Balancing the Traits

Obviously there is no way someone can be the perfect boss at all times. No matter how good you are at your job there will always be one [employee, customer, business partner] who does not like something about you; in most cases this is something you simply can not fix.

However, there are a few things a supervisor *can* control about him/herself. Namely, if you are aware of an abrasive part of your personality, an annoying speech habit, or a method of doing things that often bothers people you may be able to minimize or attempt to eliminate the negative effects it might have on how you are perceived by your co-workers. For instance: I know that I am easily frustrated in certain situations, so I can take pains to ensure my frustration at least doesn't show to those around me. Alternatively, I can monitor my own mood and ascertain when it's time to take a two-minute break to breath and let some of the stress out.

There is another generally affective form of balancing. If you are aware of something about yourself that can negatively affect your supervisory performance perhaps it can serve as an incentive to adopt more positive habits.

Let's say your habitual demeanor is somewhat off-putting and there's just no way you can change it; instead of worrying about a personality characteristic that you can't change you might worry instead about paying greater attention to problem areas in a department or setting time aside to give your team members advanced training in areas they're interested in that might help them when opportunities for promotions come along. The options for this kind of improvement are limitless and I can guarantee any workplace has areas that could benefit from special attention.

My Best Bosses

We've covered a lot of traits so far in this book - the good, the bad, the "who knows?" - and you've undoubtedly noticed some repetition about what's desirable and hopefully are not too confused about what is possible and what can be done to ensure everyone is happy. Now we're going to look at two completely outstanding bosses; these two were the best supervisors I've ever worked with and each for completely different reasons.

I worked for this first boss (we'll call her Janet) for four years and would have gladly continued in that job indefinitely if moving hadn't changed my plans. Janet was the paragon of the "strict matron" mentioned in my sketch at the beginning...she showed up for work 15 minutes early every day with her hair pulled back severely and her clothes meticulously ironed. Her voice reminded me of crunching gravel and her words had a crack in them that demanded people listen. You'd think a woman of just barely over five feet tall who supervised mainly high school students would have difficulty keeping her employees in line...and you'd be wrong.

She sounds like a fun person to work with, doesn't she? The thing about Janet is that her strict demeanor melted off almost immediately whenever she interacted with any of her team...yet she had a way about her that reminded us that the "stone-hearted boss" lay just beneath the surface, ready to be called back to light whenever needed.

Janet provided excellent training and made her expectations very clear to everyone. Unlike so many bosses I've worked with she was not afraid to tell us whenever there was a problem and set out a time frame in which she expected the problem to be fixed.

Janet's work place ran like a perfectly-oiled machine; no one called in sick or came in late if there wasn't really a good reason for it, but if there was a good reason she'd be the first to show concern and offer help. Janet also used recognition more effectively than anyone else I know; it was so rare to even see a smile from her until you got to know her that a few words of praise garnered bragging rights for a month.

Thanks mostly to her unrelenting demeanor and demands for excellence in the job there were many people who simply would not work with Janet; they thought she was mean and unfair and whatever else you can think of. If there's one thing my experience has taught me it's that this kind of weeding out isn't bad at all.

Janet's outward attitude lost quite a few employees or potential employees but in this way she made sure that she never wasted time with people who weren't willing to put everything they had into their work. Those of us that stuck with the job and measured up to Janet's expectations became like family to her and she gladly taught us everything we ever wanted to know about working effectively as a team.

The second boss (we'll call him Tom) was Janet's polar opposite. Tom showed up to work on time every day but never early, his clothes were always neat and clean but never ironed or starched to the perfection Janet was accustomed to.

Some days his hair wouldn't quite sit flat and you never knew what kind of fun tie he was going to be wearing from one day to the next. Where Janet kept things moving by dint of her powerful personality first and by amiability later, Tom always approached people with soft words and a smile.

I suppose one of the things that ensured Tom was such a successful manager is that he strove to get along with everyone. He was a supervisor at the job I mentioned before that had a rather high turnover rate of managers...well they had a high turnover rate of everyone else too.

The systematic "weeding out" that Janet employed wasn't quite as desirable in this case as the company would have quickly run out of people to replace the ones that hadn't liked the strict all-business manner of the boss. Yes, this meant we had a few sub-par workers but someone was better than no one and Tom was very skilled at keeping people satisfied in the workplace.

My favorite thing about Tom was that not only was he readily available if I needed guidance or wished to address an issue, but he also scheduled everyone in the department so there would be at least 20 minutes in which the entire team was present and could be addressed as a whole to discuss concerns, review everyone's schedules to ensure they were satisfactory and to give us a chance to offer our own ideas about how to solve various problems in our daily work.

Especially at that particular job I wasn't used to this kind of one-on-one attention and found that it really motivated me to keep working and helped keep frustration levels down because I knew I could easily take my issues to my supervisor and have them considered promptly.

The Ideal Boss?

This is it, the moment you've all been waiting for. Throughout the preceding passages you may have started feeling like there was just way too much to consider and too many variables to truly know how to become an outstanding supervisor.

My conclusion? It's not so much who the boss is or what their qualities are, it's what they can achieve in the situation they are in. We're going to take a moment to go over some of the things that are the most important for a supervisor to be able to do and why.

Communication. I've addressed multiple facets of communication in this article and all of them can be condensed down to just this...someone who is, above everything, an effective communicator. In consideration of the space I have to relate these thoughts to you I am categorizing quite a range of characteristics and abilities under this heading. Making expectations known in an effective and timely manner is probably the most important here for obvious reasons...if your team doesn't understand what they're supposed to be accomplishing they can't do it to your liking. Next it's exceedingly important to be available to answer any questions regarding those expectations; I don't mean that you have to constantly check in with your team to make sure they understood everything but at least be someplace easily accessible where they can find you right away.

Countless times I've had questions while on the job and, after a fruitless and time-wasting search for my supervisor, finally gave up in frustration and out of the need to finish everything I can in the time I have. There is one thing that began as a personal preference with me out over time I've found it really does help with the amount of work that gets done...list which expectations are your top priority.

Ordering priorities from top to bottom doesn't take very long and it can go a long way to ensuring that all the things you want to get done are completed and to keeping your team focused on the task at hand rather than worrying about everything else on that list.

When there is a problem with one of your team members (work not being completed satisfactorily, arriving late, etc.) do not be afraid to talk to them about it when the problem occurs. Sure, arriving five minutes late one day may not be a big deal but mentioning it to the employee just to let them know it was noticed is a pretty painless preventative measure.

I mentioned recognition several times previously but did not mention that recognition isn't just limited to praise but also to letting your employees know that you are keeping track of everything that happens within your jurisdiction.

Efficiency. The price of everything is going up. When prices go up the first thing business owners and managers look for are ways to reduce overhead costs in an effort to prevent diminished profits and this is probably the absolute best way to save money...find ways to do the most work with the time and people you have available.

My story about how a department that ran well on no less than four people is an excellent example...when we were forced to make do with two people work was re-organized so that it could be accomplished with the manpower we had.

Imagine if every department of every business were re-organized for maximum efficiency as a matter of course rather than a last-ditch effort to keep things afloat...and imagine how much overhead cost would be diminished by only paying the wages for the people you really need.

There are some drawbacks to only keeping the number of people you need and no more because of the many variables that could cause someone to be unavailable for work on any given day, but if you make a habit of operating so that you *could* get by with less the work won't suffer if some team members are absent and fewer employees need be on the full-time payroll.

Identifies with the Employees. I'm sure we've all had supervisors who made it very clear that they were above non-supervisory employees and, however subtly, distanced themselves from their team. In many cases this is probably unintentional distancing but it is something that should be avoided at all costs.

This ties back in to having a team that feels at ease with you and feels like they can take any issue to you and it will be considered. A lot of times a good attitude and welcoming demeanor facilitates this open communication but, as has been demonstrated in Janet's case, is not absolutely necessary to achieve the same effect. It is difficult to pinpoint exact traits that really qualify as effective in this area, but there are a few things that seem to be true most of the time.

A supervisor who is able to adapt to the temperament of their workers and the type of work situation (for example, a place that allows for "weeding out" unproductive workers as opposed to one that needs all the help it can get) is probably the biggest asset a company can possibly have.

These are the people who have really figured out what identifying with the employees means; someone who manages to assert a certain measure of authority yet can still be seen as an accessible person who is there to help and to offer solutions. A supervisor who knows how to do this becomes a part of their team and is seen as an essential part of the project as opposed to someone you report progress to.

Motivation. An excellent manager is someone who both has and inspires very high levels of motivation. We've all had those days when we're tired or feeling unchallenged and just plain don't feel like doing as much work as we know we can accomplish n a day.

The supervisor is, by definition, the person charged with keeping the level of motivation to a maximum even when their personal motivation runs low. The specifics of how to achieve this are dependent on the individual situation but it is important to attach an overall sense of urgency and personal commitment to the project at hand. This can be achieved through incentives, some form of competition, or through a sense of teamwork that holds each person accountable for the success of the project...use your imagination and find something that works for the people you work with.

Teamwork. One of the most important factors involved in creating a team rather than simply having a group of employees that happen to work in the same place is in finding common ground for every person on the team...in this case, common ground in dedication to work.

Obviously this is much easier said than done and isn't achieved quickly, but through constant work and employing all the tools that make one a good supervisor it is possible. A team is a unit in which all people are equal; to run effectively it must have a leader (the supervisor) but that leader is there mainly for organization and by merit of their exceptional problem-solving prowess.

A Positive and Productive Workplace. This last accomplishment deserves special notice because it is the ultimate goal of every supervisor and the thing that requires the most ingenuity, the most constant work and adaptation, and is the most worth the effort. All other traits and achievements aside this is what the ideal boss strives for and is capable of achieving.

Yes, it takes an inestimable amount of work but also yields the same in benefits. A positive workplace is one that is pleasant and contains people who are generally content with their work with enough challenges to keep them interested, and a productive one is one that has achieved an excellent level of efficiency and defeated the lack of motivation to deliver the best possible results to the business they work for.

In conclusion, bosses come in all shapes and sizes and can be of just about any personality type and still be effective at their work if they approach the work with dedication and an eye for improvement. Being a good supervisor isn't easy and I'm sure we've all met people who were not qualified to be in such a position, yet it doesn't take much more than simple determination and a few basic skills to have what it takes to be an outstanding boss.

David Brooke has been a motivational speaker and inspiration to many for over 30 years. Know as "The Brooker", he has overcome numerous personal tragedies to achieve fulfillment in all aspects of his life. Becoming a self made millionaire before the age of 30, set the stage for a succession of events that included being a Nordstrom store manager, a National Champion hydroplane driver, an airplane owner & pilot, and a successful business owner.

The deaths of his wife, father, mother, and sister-in-law in a short period of time would test his determination to apply all of the lessons he had been teaching since he started.

As a professional manager for his entire life, David became very passionate about the qualities that

make a "great boss" and he shares the
secrets that help you to be a better
boss as you continue on life's journey.

Website: www.thebrooker.com

E-mail: thebrooker@thebrooker.com